Forward

Eric Cram

Foreword

There is no guarantee that any of this is accurate.

I may be digging a hole on sacred ground that will need to be backfilled and atoned for.

Today's understanding may only be a vehicle delivering us to tomorrow.

The path forward may have little in common with our past. We may make many mistakes before we *arrive.*

But, so what? In our time, against our adversaries...is there another option?

Forward, no matter the cost.

...I send my messenger, and he shall prepare the way before me...

I send unto you Elijah the prophet, before the coming of the great and terrible day of Jehovah. And he shall turn the heart of the fathers to the children, and the heart of the children to their fathers, lest I come and smite the earth with a curse.

In the Beginning...

We inhabit a multidimensional realm
We create visible and invisible life and fruit
This realm is our birthright, our reward, and our responsibility
Everything needed to make it paradise is within reach

This realm is now in a state of decay, chaos, and violence
Did it begin as this, or as a peaceful flower?

Creating paradise will require Unconditional Love

[2] The Living Depth

The Genesis creation story is at least true enough
Shedding light on humanity;
Great potential, current condition, and continued struggles
It tells the story of our multidimensional realm

Not just poetic metaphor
Including space and time

A living depth beyond the known aspects

[3] The Fall

We lost touch
Parting from our living depth
Parting from *the* living depth
As within, so without

Excluding and imprisoning parts of ourselves
Exiting from essential aspects of this realm

Death by compartmentalization…

The serpent and the fruit

Tempted by the serpent's offer, Eve weakly refuses:
You do not eat of it, nor touch it, or you will die;
She misquotes God's only rule:
In the day of your eating of it, dying, you do die.

The serpent reveals himself in his response:
Dying, you do not die.

God and the serpent agree on the dying

[2]
Eve partakes; then Adam
Dying, did they die or not die?
Yes
Dying, they did die, and not die.

God speaking to and of the entire person
You: Multidimensional; across all time

You will die

The serpent speaks to and of a fraction
you: lower-dimensional, for a brief moment

you [small, lost, for now] will not die

Misidentified

God also has a whole name in the garden;
The serpent spoke only part
When Eve did not correct him
The serpent knew he won

Always addressing the partial
Always you; never You

Never addressing the Whole

Before the Serpent

Long before the serpent appeared
They wandered from the Whole self
Lacking, grasping; not Okay
Parched for reunion

Their hearts courted the fruit
Their hunger was a beacon

The serpent accepts the invitation

Premeditation

Dis-integrated forms are offered relief
With less than a nudge, they fall
Justifying their premeditated consumption;
It will not kill All of me; not now

Blame the serpent [whom we beckoned]
He snared us at the poisonous tree

[Where we lingered]

[2]
Resting innocently in this perilous place
Supine; lips parted
He blew on my hand
It grabbed and shook the tree

The fruit fell into my oblivious mouth
He outwitted us; overpowered us

Your creation was outmatched

A long fall consummated

A deeply rooted disease
Piercing up through every aspect
Unfolding in the light of day
One thousand year Fall bloomed

From One fulfilled to disjointed yearning
The story of two or humanity allegorized

How do we get home?

The grace of the tree

The tree of the Knowledge of Good and Evil
Cruel to place it within perfection
But it was not an inevitable temptation
Nor necessary for free will

The tree reflected our inner condition
Not a tool of torment

It was a mirror for the soul

[2]
Pass by: What do you feel?
The whole, healthy being smiles
And our garden is orderly and inhabited
We operate here and illuminate it

Without desire, fear or disdain
No appetite this fruit may satiate

All aspects operating and aligned

[3]
Pass by: What do you feel?
The eye is charmed by the fruit's beauty
The stomach groans for satisfaction
The mind thirsts for its knowledge

The soul shutters
Truth is not embodied

Return to abandoned wholeness

[4]
This gracious reflection
A lighthouse warning of a rocky shore
Calamity could not sneak up in its presence
Change course or be shipwrecked

Tempted through the eye, stomach and mind
Trifectas often elude to a perfect trap

They were ripe to be plucked

Self-sabotage

Abandoning certain aspects
They desired to eat the fruit
(Why not heed this warning?)
Desiring, then condemning their desirous selves

Criminal and judge sharing one body
Naked and ashamed

I cannot trust [the hollowed, small] *me* [still embodied];

[2]
The Commandment and the Tree
The gracious guide to maintain wholeness
Once a gentle reflecting pool
Degrades into a law obeyed through willpower

Using force against their own cravings
An obedient shell constraining a starving soul

To which of my throats shall I place this blade?

Away from the holy gaze

Having fallen so long ago
Existence, an unnamable endless ache
Then to bear the painful gaze of holiness?
The echo of the Wholly One surrounds us!

The Creator and his law
The Creator and *his* law

Pain twists into enmity

[2]
We would welcome toil and suffering
Consumption and endless maintenance
To be prey in a strange land
Contenders with soil and kin

Hide the Tree of Life from us
We will take this lesser path

If it grants moments of long-awaited silence

[3]
Blind the eye of God
Move beyond his sight
Where his gravity holds all together
But his light cannot reach

Darkened toil and contention
Away from illuminated exposure

To the outer ring of existence

A crucial battle is lost

Abandoning wholeness;
Choosing pain-management
When not consuming this fruit
Longing is the natural state

An endless toil never truly satisfying
The road home is too long

This is our new maintenance program

Removal from the garden

Banished from the Garden;
An official demotion
This disease's full manifestation acknowledged
Ten thousand choices delivered them here

Reduced to stewards of lesser aspects
Or contenders with them

The new way is poverty

[2]
The road home is too long
Guarded by angel and sword of flame
Reentering the Garden is to pass through fire
Painful exposure and sincere nakedness

The path to reintegration and wholeness
To bring unity to self and realm

...perhaps one of our sons will.

Invasion

The abandoned aspects;
We left a vacuum chaos fills
Simply weeds in an untended field?
Something more nefarious?

If only every failure had a serpent scapegoat...
But there *is* evidence of conscious adversaries

Invested in our fall

[2]
Forces eagerly inhabit vacuums
Warring for our entire realm
One aspect at a time
Awaiting surrender or neglect

Their insatiable appetites
Like our fallen cravings

Fill the endless void

[3] Terraform
The moon resists human habitation
Our world resists foreign occupation
Dark forces toil ceaseless and subtle
To terraform to their liking

Tread lightly or risk exposure
We dead may emerge from our graves

Awakened, all would be lost

The Sword of Accusation

Our realm cannot be taken
Only surrendered
Humanity and it's birthright;
Can a wedge be reasoned between us?

A divided house cannot stand
A divided person cannot occupy

Darkness wields the sword of Accusation

[2]
Bad human! At least unfit.

Who are [partial] you, you wicked human curse?
World destroyer   Overpopulator   Virus carrier

Who are you to feel worthy;
Qualified to inhabit this realm?
Your deepest desire is to surrender it
To serve a master!

[3]
Behold! Your need for Purpose
Dislocated without an external identity
You need a reason to live
A cause to justify your existence

This is the nature of a parasite

Slink into a corner;
More than you deserve

[4]
Accusation trapped our fathers
It ensnares us
The solution offered:
Retreat and slavery

Self-judgement compounds it
Craving; feeling guilty for our appetites

I cannot trust [the hollowed] *me* [still embodied]

Spell casting

Hollow accusations!
Lacking truth's potency
There is no meaningful impact
A repetitious barrage is necessary

Spell-casting and chanting to weary us
An endless expulsion of darkness' energy

Maintain the negative illusion

Rebutting the Accusation

...and [partial] I do desire a master
And [partial] I wish to relinquish control
...and [partial] I do feel unworthy

But the solution is not surrender
Not a deal with the serpent

Wholeness is the cure

[2]
...and [hollow] we do act poorly
Malnourished, we lust and crave
Missing our lost dimensions
The Sword of fire between us

Nutrients wafting from the initiated side
Disheartened, we envision ourselves there

Ah, to be full stewards!

[3]
Bad for Earth?
We are gluttonous We overconsume
It's true...but only to compensate
To sooth an unquenchable thirst

The answer: Tame the lesser appetites
Sober the grasping mind

A sharp pain may cure the ache

[4]
We desire healthy influence in many dimensions
Balanced in our occupation
We settle for power-lust in lesser aspects
relationships and occupations

More than visibility or influence
[lesser]we desire to dominate

A domination chain-reaction occurs

[5]
...and desire for Purpose is a snare
Only appealing to the lesser
A poor substitute for Meaning
An empty counterfeit for Conviction

When addressing the whole I
Darkness cannot make this *Purpose* claim

Conversation begins with my Whole Name

The Cycle

Accused and persuaded, we surrender an aspect
Being less, we lack
Lacking, we hunt in remaining aspects
Lustfully, futilely overconsuming

Our elders warned against this
Control yourself! did not resonate

They rarely demonstrated the higher path

[2]
Bloated and starving
Clearly, we've pillaged without justification
We lie in the trapper's net
Accusers arrive during glutton's remorse

You evil viruses don't deserve this aspect!
Bring evidence you should propagate.

Accused and persuaded we surrender again

[3]
Now we lack with fury
Malnourished; a living dying
We devour remaining aspects
Lustfully, futilely overconsume

In our perfected, manifested failure
The accusers arrive once again

Well…?

[4]
When passing through fire is *censored*
What remains for mankind?
Only the illusion of choice
Surrender more or be bulging, viral gluttons

These pathetic lies aimed at partial selves

We still have the power
This is our world

Agents of the Accuser

Deception is laborious
Needing human agents to succeed
Internalizing and repeating accusations
Toxicity amplified through human antennae

Through us the signal permeates our realm
Loveless destruction on their behalf

Banishment and retreat into smaller corners

[2]
The illusion is a convincing tide
Born submerged in this sin [misunderstanding]
Judge and convict sharing a body
Naked and ashamed

But once the signal is interrupted
This illusion vanishes instantly

Scales fall from our eyes

[3]

Go to the remote places
Alaskan wilderness and Chilean desert
Visit the Tibetan mountains, absent of agents
The empty seas where no antennae amplify

What do you hear?
What do you feel?

The scales loosen

Victory

Before One Whole Man 1000 invaders flee
A rightful and substantial heir
1000 illusory imposters
Before Holder of the Deed

1000 swimming tigers
One shark

I've come for my world

[2]
Everything favors us
The Earth
The Universe
God
All natural law

5000 Years Later...

Saving our Fathers and Mothers

Our fathers' failures fall on us
Falseness they adopted
Aspects surrendered
Battles lost

We have inherited the illness
And possibly advanced it

Judging more aspects; suppressing more

[2]
Banishing to the dungeon, we hear no cries
We hear cries
We turn away from ourselves and our birthright
Inhabiting even less of ourselves

Less perceptible and less powerful
Less access to aspects of our realm

Phantoms in our homeland

[3]
Apparitions without substance
Forest creatures barely sense us
Feeble specters; haunting facets
Unable to place a weighted hand

Phasing in and out of a dimension
Before abandoning it altogether

Existing, we do not exist

Saving our fathers and mothers

Did the ancients live to 900 years
sheltered from modern warfare's intensity?
Perhaps they did not manifest sickness and aging
as a feverish attempt to escape themselves.

Or did they borrow against their progeny
Delaying payment for ten generations

Do we pay with interest?

[2]
Our suffering cleanses their karma
Born under a mountain of debt
We must crawl our way to the surface
With one arm bound

Making peace with this limitation
We venture to rescue humanity

Inviting truth and victory

[3]
Puzzle pieces discovered
Winning lost battles
Transcend; overcome past deficiencies
Liberating humanity across time

Avoidance will only forfeit our rightful position
Passing our fathers' debt to our children

Bankruptcy looms

Regaining

We can reclaim the lost
Reintegrating toward wholeness
Allowing exposure and nakedness
Looking upon our frailty and wounds

Cut into 100 pieces;
Loving the exposed one *as-is*

Gravity fosters reconciliation

[2]
Reconciling
Gaining mass and power
Regenerating in this realm
Dwelling in a meaningful way

Lighting darkened abodes

Worthy Stewards
Trusted few pass through fire

Easing the multi-dimensional realm

[3]
Unity begets unity
Before One Whole, 1000 flee
Two disperse 10,000
Even math favors us

Our light grows exponentially brighter

The Materialist Agent

The small spaces we now inhabit!
The most ill retreat most
Embracing accusation
Groomed to surrender more

Those who have little will have less.

Materialism: A bullet looking for a target
Meaningless, valueless biology
Diminished to an empty, physical ghost
Dying, we do die

Love is only chemistry
Beauty is formulaic
Human rights are unjustified
Freedom, a construct

Why propagate? Why anything?
Irrelevant existence
Lost connection
Unjustified desire to live wains

His children have been locked in cages
They do not remain silent
Tied tightly; the undying soul
Haunting belief: No value or meaning
A glitch in evolution:
Meaninglessness, a searing pain?
What faulty gene compels us to crave more?

What mechanism of natural selection
Demands suffering escort truth?

Come steady, kindly addictions
Sing louder than the cries
And I will serve you only
Prop me up as the living

This encumbered planet—
Better off without me
Not that I should care
Neither matter

Pain creates self-hatred—illogically
More cognitive dissonance
Terror rises from the dungeon;
His *nonexistent* children

Sentimentality; a foolish religion
Why does it persist when it shouldn't?
But *shouldn't*s shouldn't exist
Then what was that?

Standing accused and convicted
From within and without
There is nowhere to go
Only *Away*

But he's afraid to embrace it
Fear of Nothingness?
Better to be tormented and living?
Then judging his own illogical cowardice

Lashing out to ease the pain
Power; a soothing balm
He writes a book or movie
He teaches and legislates

Burdening others with his painful beliefs
Infecting them with his conflict

External Power covers internal impotence

The Tech Option

Technology will soon allow even the timid to leave
Physical Aspect surrendered non-violently
Online, VR, brain-machine interfaces
A velvet noose: No bullet required

We already use surrogates
They stand between us and our senses
Mitigating damage
Dulling connection

We've embraced personas
The soul's safe bubble
Why not one more layer
One more interference?

A tech realm awaits the Accused
Eagerly ushering the Undeserving
Privilege, then Option, then Law
A specter of the ghost I once was

A phantom that can be unplugged

The Tree of the Knowledge of Good and AI-ville
Does it tempt you?
In how many ways?

Just shiny enough to convince us
Plug in for access to amazement!
Its promise will never be fulfilled
Just enough to inject fear to feed upon

Nano tech; Functional for 15 years
Then a life-long bad trip
If we remove it, you will die.
But we can sedate you.

They are one step closer
Not to success, but failure

Accusers have built-in self-sabotage...

Blueprint for Invasion

Seduction

Subtlety, when disadvantaged…
since we cling to physical aspects
Gates closed to soldiers open for teachers;
The Trojan Materialist; Anti-human

Writers, directors, marketers, and politicians
Given over to the mission of human banishment
Compelled to create an equilibrium
between their inner and outer worlds

They weave us a beautiful garment
It tightens as we stroll…

Subtle positive and negative suggestions
Design our preordained conclusion;
I shouldn't physically exist and shouldn't want to.

We fantasize 40% of our lives, and would more if we could
But jobs, tasks, and pain prevent us from living in our self-created worlds.

But what if your imagination created 100% of your life?
24 hours, 7 days; A pain-free, heavenly existence!

What is more liberating than designing your own world?
This is true Freedom!

It's time: Be relieved of this burdensome body
Embrace the next frontier; Humanity's evolution

For the heroic and truly progressive,
an indistinguishably virtual world awaits
Unlimited resources and pleasure
Validating luxuries and relationships

We can do so much more unencumbered
Life: Finally, heaven on Earth!

How do we refute this logic
How do we resist this offer
when suffering from lost identity and misplaced birthright?

Blueprint for Invasion

Intimidation

Suggestion gains steam
Power shifts in their favor
...so they would have us believe
The soft pitch is retired
A direct message emerges
Raw, violent, and voluminous
Bully the resistant into submission

What's wrong with you? You're stubborn and archaic!
Flesh is for barbarians, you gross, infectious, world-killers

Selfish; enjoy your ridicule. Hated by the masses
Abandoned technophobes conspire against progress
We will unwrite your history and dominate your progeny!

You'll fight over garbage and endure a gruesome death by barbarism
Your failing forms ravaged by disease and age!

A Response to Accusation

We see a tantalizing trade
Surrender pain; receive pleasure
Surrender poverty; receive wealth
Localized sting recedes; general ache increases

Fantasy: An oasis for the least fulfilled
The empty romance of ceding physical reality
As hollow as humanity's past retreats

Anti-transcending, anti-mastering
Anti-integrating, anti-Christ

Seduced by promised divinity
To become gods of a lesser aspect
Yet once we surrender low rank in higher dimensions
The godness quickly evaporates

Oh, to return to such impoverished richness!
To possess the aspects that pained us with exposure
Before we were failed by forbidden fruit
Before surrendering communion with our realm

We have chosen fleeting relief
Now we struggle; an existence of toil and violence
Consuming beings once like kin
Eventually consuming ourselves

Masks

And Masked

The wincing, silenced soul
Some may not understand
They feel nothing, or feel protected
And sometimes a mask is just a mask

But the dark art of manipulation
The powerful practice it

The powerless are unaware

[2]
You don't deserve to experience this world this way
Surrendering a personal aspect
Surrender a corresponding outer aspect
Cover your mouth; we steal your speech

They impose masks to diminish us
The sorcery of domination

Our submission is ritual participation

[3]
They speak out both sides:
America is an evil empire
Slavery, misogyny, consumption…
but government wouldn't mislead us

They wouldn't mask us against our interests
Not to serve themselves and amass power

Their policies are only good for us

Masked

Some prefer to be always masked
Not for protection
To avoid others' rejection
It triggers self-hatred

Recoiling
Gravitating toward diminishment

Preferring to always be masked

[2]
…and triggered by the unmasked
Healthy humanity
Powerfully masculine and feminine
Mobility exposes the bed-ridden

Avoid the light of wholeness
Painful to behold when not possessed

Force it to stop shining…

[3]
Lower the successful to my level
The hopeful, courageous, and brave
The overcomers and soul-rich
Emotional communism!

If my wounds cannot be hidden,
You, too, must act as wounded

Equality of spiritual poverty

[4]
Mask the world!
Wound them more than I
Make them destitute
So my poverty shines

Vindictive, self-hating throngs
Pained faces twisting to hatred

(In the crowd, should I raise my withered hand?)

I failed to see the signs

[5]
And the clandestine Materialist agents
Having given up so many aspects
Now lustfully consuming power
Crafting movements to arm the bitter

Through them, they impose their pain on others
Agents of agents of Accusation

Destroy it all!

Face the World

We already cover so much of ourselves
When we don't exercise exposure
Shame sets in
Now our faces...what will be left?

The high cost of appeasing the wounded
Helping them pretend they are well

Enabling is not Love

[2]
Face the world each day
Unmasked
Exercise that courage muscle
Social discomfort

Our facial expressions give us away
We wear our fear and wounds

That's okay...more than okay

[3]
Do not surrender this dimension!
With honor, uncomfortably face the world
Twinge, and be one step closer to overcoming
The lie will not outlast you

Step toward a transcendent freedom
Opening spiritual circulation

Sending waves of healing through your body and soul

Speaking

We speak!
More than socially and politically pragmatic
It is the exercise of our natural human aspects
It comes with a price

Yet silence bears a greater price
Less of each of us

Atrophy of the soul

Surrendering our world
Willfully backing into their cages

Expanding is the answer
Not contracting
Exposing
Not diminishing

Antidote

Invaders can only offer us what they possess
Only riches of the aspects they inhabit
Never greater dimensions
Not our higher aspects or ourselves

The reason they cannot say our Whole names
We are greater than they

To acknowledge Us is to be defeated

Terraforming for invaders

All platforms broadcast *Danger!*
We remain in our shells
Reactive and defensive
Protecting what is inside

Hiding the creative, deeper self
Vulnerable heads delay living in the light

Waiting for a safe moment to extend

[2]
Scooped up into different cages
For your best interest
In the name of national security
I will greet myself and the world...someday

That sun won't rise without being summoned
Turn way from fear and negativity

Emerge and the path will appear

[3] Gratitude

Relaxes the parasympathetic system
Allowing my softer self to emerge
Introducing Me to mE
Knowing can begin

Sunlight and fresh air
Work can begin

Gratitude; The antidote to fear

Authentic Light

Counterfeits shine when truth falls
True charisma and confidence dim
So little fruit remains
We follow a light without warmth

The single-mindedly wicked are appealing
Their conscience locked in the abyss

They don't wrestle

[2]
Narcissists and psychopaths
Having buried the resistance within
Moving forward unified
Shining a plagiarized light

Forged adornment

They will repay seven-fold

[3]
Yet rightness illuminates from within
Warmth and light born of oneness
A single mind
Pure or purified by fire

An undivided house;
Integrated and matured

A reconciled whole

[4]
No debt to pay
This light pays other debts
This healing heals others' wounds
An asset paying dividends

We can set this right

The Cost of Avoidance

Simulants energize the wounded
Anti-depressants offer reprieve
But the sick should be resting and healing
Not leaping on broken limbs

The debt of Avoidance
We always pay interest

A full life awaits

Lethally Embodied

Disembodied, I rattle ghostly chains for truth
Impacting with the potency of mist
Not active, powerful embodiment
The flavor of change, but no feast

Demons speak to the uninitiated:
Jesus I know, and Paul I know...but who are you?

It's best to gain substance

[2]
But embodied truth takes flowing form
A demonstration; Imparting
I am Freedom; A conduit for life
Lethally embodied; Not lacking

Neutralizing accuser and accusation
Not overconsuming; No compensating.

Chose the path of fire

The Earth Groans

Resisting foreign occupation
The earth bemoans its indigestion
Attempting to purge
To settle its stomach

Drought and famine
Hurricanes and floods

Earth awaits the return of royalty

--- --- ---

Slavery of Magnitude

The devil offers luxury and freedom
Lies of omission
The luxury of sleeping in
The freedom to avoid this life

Reclined on a luxurious mattress
Holding gold bullion in a cage

Competition and war among prisoners are acceptable.

[2] Amnesiacs
A forgetful race adopts a false identity
Accepting roles and limitations
Forgotten, neglected, surrendered
I need something more!

...but the cloak of forgetfulness...
It seems there is no more

Deluded: *We are on an island in space.*

Sword of Flame

The journey home through garden gates
Guarded by a sword of flame
The refining fire ignites our facade
Cardboard pretense exchanged for exposure

Raw feelings, beliefs, and fears
The judged within finds honesty brutal

We fear and resist our salvation

[2]
This gracious discomfort
Ending an age of endless maintenance
Then remove the warden
Release the convicts

Love the unloved
Sunlight and fresh air

Reintegrating into a society of One

[3] Substance

Aspects once bound and imprisoned
Converge and mature to equilibrium
Substance returns to the phantom
Multidimensional Man

Triggers have been detached
Sensitive explosives evaporate

Unconditional Love was always an option

[4]
I reoccupy this realm
Healing it as I am reinvigorated
I am at peace and radiate
I am in order; it resonates

All is imbued with patience and power
Land, elements, animals, and plants

The social tapestry reflects our wholeness

[5] Trustworthy
A shunned shadow hungers for love
Starvation without death
Reaching up from a living grave
Grasping at counterfeit feasts

Craving resurrection
The buried undead drive us

Dictating our path

[6]
Yet One Woman
Embodying all aspects of herself
Nothing meaningful lacks
Not tempted to overconsume

No fear a suppressed aspect will emerge
Clutching at attention and validation

She is honored with power and authority

[7]
Having fallen so far
Foreign to ourselves
The news is so good
We can't accept it all at once

The Cycle

Allowing ourselves to be loved
We reveal our deeper self
Love that self
Reveal deeper
Love that
Reveal
Love
Wholeness

The damp, dark places;
Comparted, we become strangers
Unknown is unpredictable
Aspects wither and disease grows

Courage opens the doors
Allows light and fresh air;
Revealing and embracing
Healthy aspects thrive and disease withers

...but what might we discover?
Secrets, fears, limitations
They are no threat to us
They hold the keys to the kingdom

Loving the Wounded Son

Fathers' hearts turn toward their sons

A tree does not exist to bear fruit
A tree exists
Fruit is often the natural result
Noncompulsory

As we are whole, we inhabit
Life grows in the light of our presence

Fruitfulness, order, and clarity

[2]
We are not a means to an end;
Robots built to perform a function
Our worth is not tethered to an outcome
We transcend Purpose

Love; the world-changer
is not for changing the world

Love without ambition

[3]
My son's broken leg...
We don't pretend he can walk
We don't banish him because he can't
Our happiness with him is unaffected

His worth is irreducible
He is fully invited to participate

He requires extra attention

[4]
Our family is limited
Until he heals—if ever
But we chose a wounded family
Not a broken family

Our wholeness is not in our functionality
It's in our unity

We are one

[5]
We don't pretend he isn't injured
We accept the limitation
We don't pretend he doesn't exist
We accept we are vulnerable

Wounded and discarded; the recipe for a monster
Wounded and held; how heroes are forged

We don't pretend

[6]
We don't take shortcuts
Injecting drugs for moment of strength
We don't acquire the debt of addiction
Eventually, it comes due with interest

Fleeting performance
Then greater injury and pain

No shortcuts

[7]
We don't use medicinal negativity;
The toxic ointment of scorn
A fresh blow to the head
To help forget the broken leg

A ton of negativity
An ounce of momentary change

Result is more injuries

[8]
We don't use medicinal positivity
To heal or motivate
Encouragement, acceptance, or validation;
Empty and unilluminated

Teaching how to lie with false love
All future complements become suspect

The blind will forth love without loving

[9]
We deeply know him, so we love him
Mysterious goodness is his essence
His eternal value is unconditional
So is loving him

This powerful demonstration springs forth
Allowing it, not willing it

There is no feigning this transcendent state

Atonement

I have banished many children
Flesh of my flesh
Denying them a place and name
Accepting only a strong few

The world teems with those I have not loved
Understandably short-sighted

But there are some I have kept from being loved

[2]
Apology can't repair this transgression
This harm of a sacred creation
It can't be undone
It can be healed

Grieving is a demonstration of love
Mourning bears witness to value

It is an honor to atone

[3]
As long as it takes
Cleaning up the mess I've made
To reestablish relationship
Bearing witness to the injustice

A creation has been wronged
It is an honor to atone

As long as it takes

[4]
Obscured by the tree line
Come forth from the wilderness
Let not one more moment pass
Come gather around the fire

Let me know you
Know me

I'll give you a name

[5]
Your jagged teeth don't offend me
Uncouth and unsocialized
Grow, if you grow
Be who you are

More children emerge
Named in the warm glow

Heal, if you heal

We are One

Parenting

We have always been our own parents,
taking cues from our those that raise us
We internalize or reject their examples
Values, love, and expectations

But we are the gatekeepers
We can change it all

We decide

Aging

The Gravity of Wholeness

Gravity draws each toward Wholeness
But what devious aspects will emerge?
Does a shadowy virus await contact
Invoking an eternal fate worse than death?

Loveless walls prevent infection
Labor intensive; controlling by withholding

Resistance is my top priority

[2]
Second, maintaining a personable facade
Devoted, I offer sacrifices of energy
A hotel facia with smiling mannequins
Concealing a prison of non-integration

Yet, aging, my energy recedes
I divert from auxiliary functions;

Happiness, connection, service...*shutting down*

[3]
Weakening further, the facade fails
Prison guards are exposed
I am a repetitive, negative mouthpiece;
My fears and resistance

This is also grace
A last chance to unite

Soon the sun sets

[4]
A soul's ice age approaches
We will sleep with open eyes
In changeless time, no growth occurs...
Then consequences be damned!

With crashes of chaotic thunder
All prisoners flood the yard

Sooner would have been better

[5]
Youth wasted resisting wholeness
We can't do it forever
The blessing of failing walls
This irresistible tide comes

We might as well love now!

vs. Freedom

False Freedom

Do as I wish…
unaware of my desires
Do as I choose…
from preprogrammed options

Free to cut myself into pieces
Free to drown out the painful cries

Half a man, free to become a quarter

[2]
Free to serve many brutal masters
To indulge our deadly parasites
Surrendering higher dimensions
Allowing overgrowth of chaos and darkness

Then slash and burn in lesser dimensions
As we retreat even from them

The freedom to blindly occupy a shrinking cage

True Freedom

Expansion!
This world is my home
I go where I chose
Dwelling in mysterious dimensions

Watch how the thunder strikes
Feel the rain I formed

Feared gods have become tools in my hand

[2]
Leveling mountains of discontent
I am springs in the desert
Turning wastelands into plush valleys
I am Free to heal the Earth

Exchanging defense for offense
Turning from self-inflicted pain
Occupying the entirety of our realm
Uniting order and unknown

Fully becoming; being who I am
Fully expressing who I am

Why not?

Embodied Existence

I am flawed and unashamed
Vulnerable and celebrated
I fail; there is no judge
Exposed and will not hide

Every shattered child, come dine
Wild ones, come exhibit

I exist; I am not sorry

[2]
Cryptic expression;
Unnamable feelings
Drawing water
Drawing blood

Entangled in multidimensional existence
I see you rise and breathe

Another wave comes to submerge you

[3]
You overwhelm some aspects
Well-harnessed in others
Others sleep with you by their side
Soul; an enigmatic, irreducible recipe

Dreaming my dreams
Explosive and healing

Holier than I; how do I sit in judgment?

[4]
Illuminating my cowardice
Yet *I* am *your* guardian?
How should I be your gatekeeper?

Long before you surrender
I will fail, as these bars

[5] Water

I attempt to gather you as water in a fishing net
Else you may flow toward storm drains
Seeking low ground where disease resides
The shortest path back to the ocean source

Into obscurity, losing identity
Salted, absorbed, and consumed

Is that home?

[6]

Mother Ocean, Receive me into the vastness!
I may rise and contribute within a thousand rain drops
Each one falling into a receptive womb
Named as if a word could contain you

Unacknowledged, I live in their unnamable desires
Their unquenchable spirit

The explosive protest for soulful life

[7]
Mother Ocean received many
They evaporated and contributed
Collected into Me
I fell into a willing womb

Sacred mystery born into confusion
Honor to the ancestors

Here I am

Cryptography

Cryptic expression, unnamable feeling
Wild will of irrepressible beauty
Come share this space
I swept it for you

The floor creaks
Can you find your way in?

We keep missing each other

[2]
I'm learning your language
Deeds, not words
I can always start right where I am
Choosing to let you blaze, even if I am tinder

I will not poison you with discomfort
Except when I do

Division; an insanity I allow to untangle

[3]
I am not a virus
I am not a plague
I am not bad for Earth
The air I exhale gives life!

The end of recoiled posture
No more corner living

Expanding, I fill the world with life

[4]
Consumption is not my nature
I shine and am fruitful
I am not a parasite
My presence more than compensates

The immunity to greed is not guilt or shame
We are immunized by expansion into all our aspects

Integrate; "I am of God."

[5]
I exist; I am not ashamed!
Attempting to condemn me
My enemies become vulnerable
Exposing their positions

Surrounded on all sides
I see faces in every direction

...my prey delivers itself to me ☺

Perfect Lineage

I am Man...of Man
Son of deputized Mankind
An unbroken lineage
Who are *you*?

My blood—of mankind
It is my witness

Authority flows through me

[2] Faith
This awareness; this experience
The faith that moves mountains
Not *trust* or *belief*
It is *Have* or *Have Not*

Substantial faith, not ethereal
A matter of ownership, not will

To have faith is to possess

[3]
Many may claim sonship to God
Scattered across dimensions
But who has dominion here and now?
Man, Son of Man

Rid of the spell of *puny, sinful humans*
Cast off cowering before an angry, disappointed God

We are Mankind!

[4]
Man, of Mankind; god, of God
To the thousands about to take flight:
You're in the wrong house
If I turn and see you, I'll tear you apart.

Kicking in the door, life and healing rush through
Unseen dimensions open and receive

We inhabit previously forbidden aspects

[5]
Something scatters when illuminated
Who is my accuser?
I integrate; it vanishes
Where is the resistance?

Present. Sober. Aware.
Reoccupy the aspects

I am the breath of God

Who Dares?

This world carries momentum
Spinning at 1000 miles an hour
We like it this way
We intend to keep it

So you, roaring like a lion
But slapping at us with a baby's hand
You, limp-wristed, sulking disembodied

Who are you?

[2]
Cowering in the dark places
Seducing our wounded
Latching to the lost
Offering false solace if they betray

Who are *you*, that we should provide shelter?
You failed your world; go earn it back

You stand accused

[3]
Let the judges of the realm
Of light and dark
Of beauty, chaos, and spirits of the air
Let them convene and listen

Yet, should corruption endure
If their wisdom or constitution fails

The Son of Man will remain

[4]
Assemble all armies against us
In one land, for your greatest battle
Erect impenetrable walls around the arena
Where no man can escape

March in and fill the land with dragons
Demonstrate your greatest strength

And you will see who is trapped with whom

[5]
Rise with razor teeth, beast of the underworld!
From below, devour this alien force
Discharge their bones
Let their decomposition nurture our soil

If the beast fails to waken and feed
Then with a sword we will slay each invader

Your pleas will become the songs of our children

Here I Am

Here I am
Demonstrating unrealized dimensions
Holding riches in an open hand
Come and see

This way
Walk out of the cage

Shedding counterfeits like dust

Love; disruptive technology
Destroying this system's monopoly:
Magnitude and lustful consumption
Diluted satisfaction

But multidimensional fulfillment...
Jesus brought; The prophets bring

I see scriptures in this light

You will see a loving God
Only shaking us to wake us
Our discomfort is ours
Fear of leaving our cells

Hunting by scent;
An unseen treasure

To breathe is to know the way

Courage is required
Resisting fear of the unknown
If the terrain was familiar
This would already be ours

Only the unknown remains
Only the unknown will satisfy

Let us draw the whole world into ourself!

www.ingramcontent.com/pod-product-compliance
Lightning Source LLC
LaVergne TN
LVHW041129150826
845673LV00007B/2246

* 9 7 8 0 9 8 4 5 3 4 7 0 8 *